ALL ABOUT

BTS

Quizzes, QUOTES, QUESTIONS, and MORE!

BY ARIE KAPLAN

ILLUSTRATED BY Risa Rodil

Grosset & Dunlap

GROSSET & DUNLAP
An imprint of Penguin Random House LLC, New York

First published in the United States of America by Grosset & Dunlap,
an imprint of Penguin Random House LLC, New York, 2024

Text copyright © 2024 by Arie Kaplan
Illustrations copyright © 2024 by Risa Rodil

Photo credits: used throughout: (abstract scribble lines) pixaroma/iStock/
Getty Images, (abstract geometric shapes) RLT_Images/DigitalVision
Vectors/Getty Images, (abstract star, flower, cross shapes) Spicy Truffel/
iStock/Getty Images, (night cityscape) halepak/DigitalVision Vectors/
Getty Images; 13, 29, 45, 61, 73: (speech bubbles with question marks)
Oleksandr Melnyk/iStock/Getty Images; 14, 30, 46, 62, 74: (finger heart)
innni/iStock/Getty Images

GROSSET & DUNLAP is a registered trademark
of Penguin Random House LLC.

Visit us online at penguinrandomhouse.com.

Manufactured in Canada

ISBN 9780593754672   10 9 8 7 6 5 4 3 2 1 FRI

Design by Kimberley Sampson

TABLE OF CONTENTS

Part 1

PUTTING THE GROUP TOGETHER
More Than Just a Boy Band

They're singers, dancers, rappers, songwriters, and award winners. Their names are RM, Jin, Suga, V, J-Hope, Jimin, and Jungkook. And together, they're the legendary South Korean boy band BTS.

However, calling BTS a boy band isn't really doing them justice. They're more than that. They're icons, and they've consistently broken records worldwide, in terms of concert revenue, video streams, and social media engagement.

But how did these young men become the force of nature known as BTS? And what makes them different than other Korean pop stars? Read on and find out!

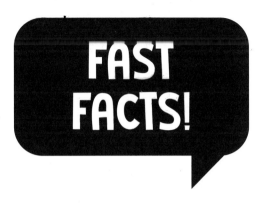

In 2018, BTS performed at the *Billboard Music Awards* (BBMAs).

That year, the BBMAs were held at the MGM Grand Garden Arena in Las Vegas.

The Hitman and the Monster

Bang Si-hyuk had a dream. As a music producer for actor and singer Park Jin-young's JYP label, Bang was a successful figure in the Korean pop—or "K-pop"—world. He was even known as "Hitman" because of the many hit records he produced for K-pop artists like the boy band g.o.d.

But as much as he enjoyed his work for JYP, Bang really wanted to try making it on his own. To do this, in 2005, he built a company called Big Hit Entertainment.

In 2010, Bang had an idea for a hip-hop group centered around the talents of rapper Kim Namjoon, who was professionally known as "Rap Monster" and later simply "RM."

With RM as the leader of this new hip-hop group, Bang set about finding the other members.

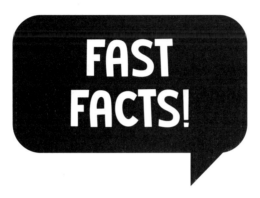

FAST FACTS!

One of the most popular songs Bang Si-hyuk wrote for g.o.d. was the 1999 hit "One Candle."

Bang also wrote the hit song "Like the First Time" for the girl group T-ara in 2009.

The Bulletproof Boy Scouts

After RM signed with Big Hit, Bang Si-hyuk soon recruited Min Yoongi—who went by the stage name "Suga"—for his new hip-hop group. Then he signed dancer and rapper Jung Hoseok (J-Hope), singer Kim Seokjin (Jin), vocalist and rapper Jeon Jungkook, vocalist Kim Taehyung (aka V), and finally, dancer and singer Park Jimin.

In South Korea, pop stars are often known as "idols," and pop groups are known as "idol groups." And even though Bang Si-hyuk originally envisioned BTS as a hip-hop group, he quickly rebranded them as an idol group because he thought they would be more commercially successful that way.

Bang called his idol group "Bangtan Sonyeondan" (in English: "Bulletproof Boy Scouts"). Although fans sometimes call them "The Bangtan Boys," the group is often simply known as "BTS."

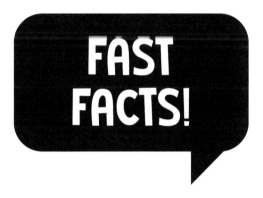

FAST FACTS!

Kim Taehyung chose "V" as his stage name because it stood for "Victory."

Under Bang's supervision, all seven members of BTS lived together and practiced together.

A New Kind of Idol

Before BTS came along, most twenty-first-century idol groups were friendly but bland. They were often blank slates who never sang songs about their personal struggles or about serious societal issues.

By founding BTS, Bang Si-hyuk changed all of that. The young men of BTS were partially chosen because they had strong, sympathetic personalities both in private and onstage. They were people audiences could relate to.

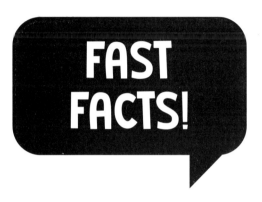

FAST FACTS!

Bang Si-hyuk admitted to sometimes feeling insecure about his work.

Because of that, Bang liked performers who weren't afraid to express their true personalities and anxieties.

Did You Know That . . .

1 RM is the only member of BTS who can speak fluent English.

2 He taught himself English by watching the American sitcom *Friends*.

3 When Suga started out as an underground rapper, he called himself "Gloss."

4 This stage name was the English translation of his real name, "Yoongi."

5 J-Hope started out as a street dancer.

6 The difference between BTS and other Korean boy bands was even reflected in their name.

7 Bang called them "Bulletproof Boy Scouts" because their toughness and resilience made them "bulletproof."

8 Back when BTS was first formed, it was rare for members of an idol group to emphasize their struggles.

9 In the early days of their existence as an idol group, the members of BTS practiced and rehearsed for twelve to fifteen hours each day.

10 Bang encouraged the members of BTS to publicly discuss the pressures of celebrity—in both their songs and in the press—which was a rarity for an idol group.

Out of Pure Enjoyment

"It's still unbelievable that our singing and dancing, which we began out of pure enjoyment, has spread such an impact across the world."

—J-Hope on his enjoyment of singing and dancing

What do *you* enjoy doing? It could be a hobby, a sport, a class at school, or something else entirely. Write about it on the lines below.

_____

_____

_____

_____

_____

_____

_____

_____

_____

_____

_____

_____

_____

_____

_____

_____

_____

_____

_____

_____

Stage Name

Some of the members of BTS use stage names. For instance, Suga's real name is Min Yoongi. "Suga" is his *stage name*. If you had a stage name, what would it be? Write about your stage name—and why you chose it—on the lines below.

_____

_____

_____

_____

_____

_____

_____

_____

_____

_____

_____

_____

_____

_____

_____

_____

_____

Quiz: Get to Know the Boys of BTS

1) In 2016, ____ released a solo mixtape called *Agust D.*

   a. Ed Sheeran
   b. Edward Sheeran
   c. Suga
   d. Eddie Sheeran

2) ____ is the oldest member of the group.

   a. Jin
   b. Bugs Bunny
   c. Mickey Mouse
   d. Woody Woodpecker

3) When ____ was a child, he was a big fan of the book *Twenty Thousand Leagues Under the Sea.*

   a. Peter Parker
   b. Miles Morales
   c. Miguel O'Hara
   d. J-Hope

4) **____ was trained in modern dance before he joined BTS.**

    a. Robby the Robot
    b. Jimin
    c. C-3PO
    d. Data

5) **____ was first discovered on a Korean reality television show called *Superstar K*.**

    a. Jungkook
    b. Marvin the Martian
    c. Stitch
    d. Yoda

Check your answers on page 78!

Part II

MAKING A NAME FOR THEMSELVES

"Skool" Starts

On June 12, 2013, BTS officially launched with their debut album *2 Cool 4 Skool*. The project wasn't a *full* album; rather, it boasted a mere seven tracks, and therefore was an "extended play" album. An extended play, or EP, is shorter than a full-length album, but contains more than a single song.

The standout song on that album was "No More Dream," which dealt with the anxiety young people feel when faced with their parents' expectations. Back in 2013, the psychological struggles and mental health issues of young people were topics that were usually considered off-limits by other idol groups. With "No More Dream," BTS set themselves apart from the rest of the pack.

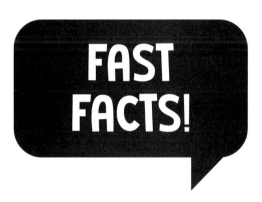

FAST FACTS!

Despite Bang Si-hyuk's desire to move BTS away from being a hip-hop group and refocus the boy band as more of an idol group, "No More Dream" was strongly influenced by hip-hop.

When BTS released their first album, it was rare for an idol group to be so overtly indebted to hip-hop music.

Their Full-Length Debut

Not long after they dropped *2 Cool 4 Skool*, BTS released two more albums: *O!RUL8,2?* (released in September 2013), and *Skool Luv Affair* (released in February 2014). But both were extended play albums. Would BTS ever release something more ambitious than an EP?

By August of 2014, the general public found out. That was when BTS released their first full-length studio album, *Dark & Wild*. Not only was the album a hit, but the Bangtan Boys also went on their first international concert tour to promote it.

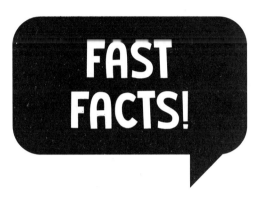

The appropriately named *Dark & Wild* was somewhat dark, as it explored themes of loss and love.

The *Dark & Wild* album cover featured a disclaimer below the title, which read (in all caps): "WARNING! LOVE HURTS, IT CAUSES ANGER, JEALOUSY, OBSESSION, WHY DON'T U LOVE ME BACK?"

The Most Beautiful

In April of 2015, BTS released their latestEP, which was titled *The Most Beautiful Moment in Life, Pt. 1*. As you may have noticed from the "Pt. 1" in the title, this was the first of three albums in BTS's *The Most Beautiful Moment in Life* (*TMBMIL*) cycle.

In May of 2015, shortly after the debut of *The Most Beautiful Moment in Life, Pt. 1*, BTS spent two consecutive weeks in the top spot of China's Gaon Weibo Chart. And in June 2015, the United States–based television network Fuse TV dubbed *The Most Beautiful Moment in Life, Pt. 1* one of the best albums of the year so far. Clearly, the group was becoming more well-known outside of South Korea.

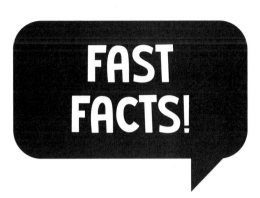

FAST FACTS!

The Most Beautiful Moment in Life, Pt. 1 has less of a hip-hop vibe and more of a pop sound, compared to BTS's previous albums.

The lead single on *The Most Beautiful Moment in Life, Pt. 1* was "I Need U."

The Cycle Continues

On November 30, 2015, seven months after they released *The Most Beautiful Moment in Life, Pt. 1*, BTS dropped the next album in the cycle, *The Most Beautiful Moment in Life, Pt. 2*. Eight of the tracks on that album charted on *Billboard*'s World Digital Songs chart.

And about a mere six months after the debut of *Pt. 2*, BTS released the two-volume album *The Most Beautiful Moment in Life: Young Forever*, which featured remixes from the first two *TMBMIL* albums, as well as three new tracks.

Perhaps the most critically acclaimed new song on *Young Forever* is "Save Me," which at first might seem like a happy song because it's set to a bouncy electropop beat. However, if you listen to its lyrics, you discover that it's actually a rather melancholy song about being lonely and craving personal connection.

By late 2015, BTS was a respected idol group known for its complex, layered songs and angst-ridden (often dark) lyrics. The Bangtan Boys had firmly established themselves. But where would their musical journey take them next?

FAST FACTS!

The three new tracks on *Young Forever* landed on the top three spots of the *Billboard* World Digital Songs chart.

This was a first for a K-pop group.

Did You Know That . . .

1 When they made their debut in public as a group in June 2013, the members of BTS were sometimes photographed wearing black bandanas and gold chains.

2 It is then fitting that the album cover for *2 Cool 4 Skool* is all black, with the word "BTS" etched in gold.

3 *Skool Luv Affair* gave BTS their first number-one nomination on a weekly music television show.

4 The TV show was called *Inkigayo*.

5 And they were nominated on *Inkigayo* for the song "Boy in Luv."

6 "Boy in Luv" is an enthusiastic love ballad.

7 In fact, "Boy in Luv" is less aggressive and confrontational than much of the music the Bangtan Boys had made prior to its release.

8 O!RUL8,2? featured the song "N.O," which criticized the societal pressures put on young people.

9 This continued the theme of social commentary in their music, which BTS established with their first ever single "No More Dream" (which appeared on *2 Cool 4 Skool*).

10 The Gaon Weibo Chart was a weekly music chart that ranked the top ten K-pop groups in China based on the social media platform Weibo.

TOP 100

☆ ① BTS

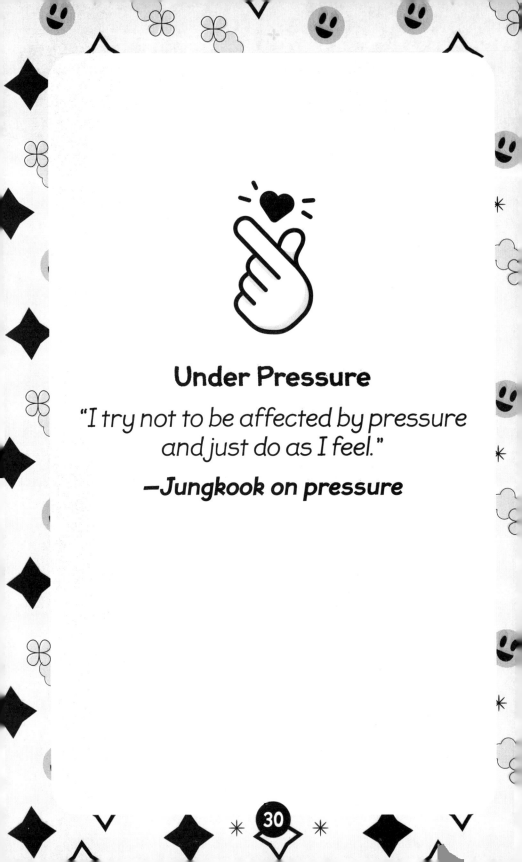

Under Pressure

"I try not to be affected by pressure and just do as I feel."

—Jungkook on pressure

Have you ever felt like you were under a lot of pressure? What did you do to relieve the pressure and feel more relaxed? Did you take a deep breath? Did someone else help you to relax? If so, who helped you during this difficult time? Write about it on the lines below.

_____

_____

_____

_____

_____

_____

_____

_____

_____

_____

_____

_____

_____

_____

_____

_____

_____

_____

Take Your Pick

The boys of BTS each have their own specialty. Some members of the group prefer rapping. Others prefer singing. Still others prefer dancing. If you were a member of BTS, which would *you* prefer? Write about your choice on the lines below.

_____

_____

_____

_____

_____

_____

_____

_____

_____

_____

_____

_____

_____

_____

_____

_____

_____

_____

_____

Quiz: Making It Happen

1) Together, *2 Cool 4 Skool*, *O!RUL8,2?*, and *Skool Luv Affair* are known as the School trilogy, which is BTS's first ____.

   a. Mummy
   b. Vampire
   c. Era
   d. Werewolf

2) BTS fans are known as ARMYs. The initials "ARMY" stand for ____.

   a. Antique Radishes are Mighty Yummy
   b. Adorable Representative MC for Youth
   c. Antique Racecars Mach-5 Yesterday
   d. Antique Radios Mixed with Yogurt

3) Jin is a ____.

   a. Foodie
   b. Puppeteer
   c. Animatronic puppeteer
   d. Puppetry teacher

4) When it comes to his clothing, J-Hope is known for being very ____.

a. Covered in plaid
b. Covered in khaki
c. Fashionable
d. Covered in corduroy

5) Aside from his work as a singer and dancer, V is also a ____.

a. Starship captain
b. Intergalactic bounty hunter
c. Alien overlord
d. Photographer

Check your answers on page 78!

Part III

GLOBAL SUCCESS AND NEW HORIZONS

Flying Higher

Thanks to BTS's world tour to promote *The Most Beautiful Moment in Life, Pt. 2*, the album rose to number one on six international music charts.

Their next album, 2016's *Wings*, continued their forward momentum as a global pop sensation. *Wings* was BTS's first original album to debut on both the *Billboard* 200 charts (in the US) and the *Billboard* Canadian Albums chart. *Wings* also included seven solo songs, one for each member of the group.

For instance, in Jungkook's solo song, "Begin," he expresses his gratitude for his bandmates. The song is an ode to empathy, as Jungkook sings of his fellow members' struggles and says that he feels their pain.

FAST FACTS!

Most of the songs on *Wings* were cowritten by the members of BTS themselves.

The songs on *Wings* delved into serious themes like emotional growth and temptation.

All About "Her"

By the time BTS's *Love Yourself: Her* album came out in September 2017, the public perception of this very unique boy band began to change. They began receiving more serious attention from music critics and other media personalities.

And now, several albums deep into their career, they were finally thought of as a musical act that had real staying power. Indeed, RM once described the release of *Love Yourself: Her* as the beginning of a new chapter in BTS's career.

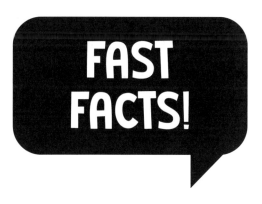

FAST FACTS!

In 2017, BTS sang one of the songs from *Love Yourself: Her* at the American Music Awards.

The song they sang at the 2017 AMAs was "DNA."

An Ode to Self-Love

The second *Love Yourself* album, titled *Love Yourself: Tear*, was released in May 2018. It was the first BTS album to debut at number one on US album charts, which was an important milestone for the group.

And as with many of BTS's previous albums (e.g., *Dark & Wild* and *Wings*), there's a serious side to *Love Yourself: Tear*. Many of the songs on this album—like "Fake Love"—are full of messages about self-love, self-esteem, and emotional resilience.

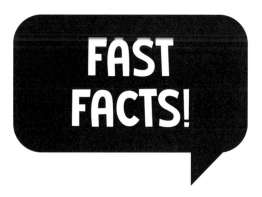

FAST FACTS!

One of the most memorable songs on *Love Yourself: Tear* was the superhero-themed "Anpanman."

One of the music videos for "Anpanman" was shot with GoPro-like cameras on a giant moon bounce (similar to a bouncy castle).

The End of an Era

The third and final album in the *Love Yourself* trilogy, *Love Yourself: Answer*, dropped in August 2018, a mere three months after its predecessor. *Answer* featured songs from the previous two BTS albums as well as eight new tracks.

Love Yourself: Answer was both a critical and commercial hit, receiving rave reviews from respected publications like *Billboard* and *Clash*.

And so ended the Love Yourself trilogy, which was BTS's fourth musical era, after the School trilogy, The Most Beautiful Moment in Life trilogy, and the all-too-brief Wings era. What would BTS do next?

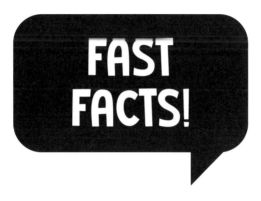

FAST FACTS!

Love Yourself: Answer was the first K-pop album to spend a year on the *Billboard* 200 chart.

It was also BTS's first gold album, with half a million certified units sold in 2018.

Did You Know That . . .

1 In 2017, BTS underwent a slight rebrand.

2 As part of that rebrand, the initials "BTS" would *still* stand for "Bulletproof Boy Scouts," but "BTS" would *also* stand for "Beyond the Scene."

3 When BTS sang "DNA" at the American Music Awards in 2017, they became the first K-pop group to perform at the major American awards show.

4 Also in 2017, *Love Yourself: Her* was the highest-charting Korean album (at the time) to make it onto the *Billboard* 200 albums chart.

5 The song "Anpanman" was about the superhero character Anpanman, which was created by Japanese cartoonist Takashi Yanase in the 1970s for a series of picture books.

6 The *Anpanman* books were adapted into a television series, which was produced in Japan beginning in the late 1980s.

7 The *Anpanman* television series became popular in Korea in the 1990s.

8 Between the first and second *Love Yourself* albums, BTS released a nine-minute video titled *Euphoria: Theme of Love Yourself Wonder*.

9 This led some to believe that their second *Love Yourself* album was going to be called *Love Yourself: Wonder*.

10 By June 2021, *Love Yourself: Answer* had become the first album by a South Korean musical act to spend one hundred weeks on the *Billboard* 200.

All Over the World

"When we began touring and performing in front of live audiences all over the world, we felt that we had evolved one step further in our journey as artists."

—Suga on touring all around the world

What do you think it would be like to go on tour all over the world? Would it be fun? Or would it be too exhausting to be worth it? Write about it on the lines below.

_____

_____

_____

_____

_____

_____

_____

_____

_____

_____

_____

_____

_____

_____

_____

_____

_____

_____

_____

Dream Vacation

Have you ever been to another country, or even another state? If so, what was that like? If you've never traveled outside of your hometown, where would you *like* to go? Where would you go on your dream vacation? Write about it on the lines below.

_____

_____

_____

_____

_____

_____

_____

_____

_____

_____

_____

_____

_____

_____

_____

_____

Quiz: International Stars

1) The BTS song "DNA" was recorded in both Korean and ____.

   a. Japanese
   b. Klingon
   c. Vulcan
   d. Romulan

2) At the *Billboard* Music Awards in 2018, the boys of BTS met ____.

   a. Barbie
   b. Taylor Swift
   c. Ken
   d. Skipper

3) Which BTS member became a member of UNICEF's Honors Club for his charitable donation to that organization?

   a. The Green Goblin
   b. Doc Ock
   c. Jin
   d. Mysterio

4) BTS's reality show ____ depicts the group traveling to places like New Zealand and Hawaii.

a. Sesame Street
b. Barney & Friends
c. Bluey
d. BTS: Bon Voyage

5) When did BTS first appear on Saturday Night Live?

a. 2019
b. 1066
c. 1776
d. 1890

Check your answers on page 78!

Part IV

MORE AMBITIOUS, MORE PERSONAL
A Constant Evolution

BTS was now a world-famous entertainment powerhouse. International audiences gravitated to their uncensored attitude and unique sound. The Bangtan Boys responded to their spike in popularity by making a type of music they'd never attempted before.

The albums BTS made directly after the Love Yourself era would be more conceptual, more ambitious, and in many ways, more personal than their previous work.

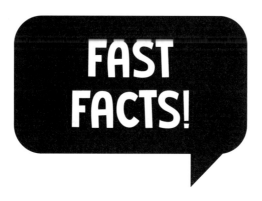

FAST FACTS!

In 2019, BTS appeared in *Time* magazine's "Time 100," a list of the one hundred most influential people who impacted society during the previous year.

The "Time 100" article about BTS was written by their fellow pop star Halsey.

Chronicle of an Idol Group

BTS's next album, *Map of the Soul: Persona*, was released in April 2019. An EP consisting of seven tracks, it was a solid album that won the group a rave review from *New Musical Express (NME)*. The second album of this era, *Map of the Soul: 7*, was released in February 2020. A full-length album consisting of songs from *Persona* as well as several new tracks, it was praised by the *Los Angeles Times*.

Although both albums were acclaimed by critics, that's far from the most important thing about them. In their *Map of the Soul* albums, the Bangtan Boys began venturing into bold new territory. That's because songs like "Dionysus" (featured on both albums) and "Interlude: Shadow" (from *Map of the Soul: 7*) were about what it was like to be an idol group.

For instance, in "Dionysus," the group meditates on the nature of celebrity and artistic integrity. This sort of meta-commentary was new for BTS, and the Map of the Soul era was their most ambitious one yet.

FAST FACTS!

On *Map of the Soul: 7*, Halsey was featured on the BTS song "Boy With Luv."

And famed pop star Sia was featured on *Map of the Soul: 7*'s final track, "ON."

This New Reality

The two *Map of the Soul* albums weren't BTS's only foray into more personal work. In November 2020, they released *Be*, which is considered by some fans to be the group's "quarantine album." That's because it was released during the start of the COVID-19 pandemic, and the songs on the album comment on the "new normal" that was established amid quarantine.

For instance, the hopeful, uplifting song "Life Goes On" was meant to give strength to people during hard times. But the whole album serves that function. A press release accompanying the release of *Be* explained that the album was designed to be a "message of healing" during the global pandemic.

FAST FACTS!

Like many of BTS's other songs, "Life Goes On" has a mix of Korean and English lyrics.

However, the song "Dynamite" (the final track on *Be*) was the group's first song to be recorded completely in English.

Victory Lap

Some might argue that—since the very beginning of their career—the boys of BTS have been running toward greater and greater success. But in 2022, the Bangtan Boys released an album called *Proof*. If their entire career is a marathon, *Proof* was a victory lap, reflecting on their past and present, and gazing toward the future.

Far from a mere "greatest hits" compilation album, *Proof* is a three-disc album that does indeed contain many of their greatest hits, especially on disc one. But disc two is chock-full of B-sides and handpicked solo numbers. And disc three boasts several unreleased songs, as well as demo versions of existing BTS tracks.

By including all of this previously unheard material, BTS pulled back the curtain, letting their fans see (or, more accurately, hear) a bit of their creative process. In this way, they continued their trend of creating increasingly personal and ambitious projects.

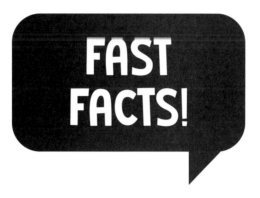

FAST FACTS!

One of the brand-new tracks on *Proof* is the album's lead single, "Yet to Come (The Most Beautiful Moment)."

Proof's closing track, "For Youth," features a live clip of BTS—and their fans—coming together to sing their 2016 anthem "Epilogue: Young Forever."

Did You Know That . . .

1 The theme of "running" occasionally surfaces in BTS's body of work.

2 *The Most Beautiful Moment In Life, Pt. 2* even includes a song called "Run."

3 The song "Tomorrow" (from 2014's *Skool Luv Affair*) includes a lyric that translates in English as: "I have a long way to go, but why am I running in place?"

4 And since 2015, BTS has had their own self-produced variety show called *Run BTS!*

5 When it comes to BTS, the term "ARMY" is often used interchangeably with "fans."

6 In late December 2019, in New York City's Times Square, BTS fans—aka ARMY—waited in line for days to ring in 2020 with their favorite idol group at *Dick Clark*'s *New Year*'s *Rockin*' *Eve*.

7 By including the live clip of their fans on the song "For Youth," BTS was making a statement about their commitment to ARMY.

8 One of the songs on *Proof* was a remastered version of the 2013 "unreleased" track "Born Singer."

9 In July of 2013, "Born Singer" was released unofficially for free downloads.

10 However, prior to its appearance on *Proof*, the song had never appeared on any of BTS's albums.

Keep Getting Up

"The song talks about how there might be unintentional mistakes and setbacks but we will keep getting up and keep on running."

—RM speaking about the song "Jamais Vu" (from *Map of the Soul: Persona*)

Has there ever been a time when you've experienced a setback or a mistake? Who helped you get back up and keep going? A friend? A classmate? A family member? Write about this experience on the lines below.

_____

_____

_____

_____

_____

_____

_____

_____

_____

_____

_____

_____

_____

_____

_____

_____

_____

_____

_____

Fashion Sense

Each member of BTS has their own unique sense of style. If you were a pop star, how would *you* dress? Write about it on the lines below.

_____

_____

_____

_____

_____

_____

_____

_____

_____

_____

_____

_____

_____

_____

_____

_____

_____

Super Quiz: Complete the BTS Banger

Okay, you've made it through all the *other* quizzes in this book so far. But this one's a bit different. As an ARMY, you know the words to every BTS song, right? Let's see just how well you know them! Fill in the blanks below to complete these BTS lyrics:

1) "I changed everything, just for ____"

   a. juice
   b. you
   c. moose
   d. Dr. Seuss

2) "In a world where you feel ____, you gotta stay gold"

   a. cold
   b. headachy
   c. clammy
   d. feverish

3) "I want a big house, big ____, and big rings"

   a. roof on the house

b. chimney on the house

c. door on the house

d. cars

4) "When I'm with you, I'm in ____"

a. New Jersey

b. utopia

c. Old Jersey

d. Just Plain Jersey

5) "Jump up to the top, ____"

a. Toe-Tapper

b. Jump-Topper

c. Tip-Topper

d. LeBron

Check your answers on page 78!

Part V

CHARTING THE COURSE

The Bangtan (Semi-Cinematic) Universe

If you've consumed a steady diet of BTS music videos—beginning with 2015's video for "I Need U"—you may have noticed that these videos connect to one another. They function like chapters in a larger story. There's a sprawling, interconnected narrative at work here, and it's called the Bangtan Universe (or "BU" for short).

But the BU isn't limited to their music videos. It also continues in BTS's "highlight reels" (a series of short films launched in 2017 to promote their Love Yourself era), and chunks of the BU narrative can also be found in their 2019 book *The Notes 1*, their *Save Me* webtoon (also from 2019), and 2020's *BTS Universe Story* mobile game.

In the Bangtan Universe's narrative, the basic storyline tells of seven young men who are friends in high school before they have a falling-out and go their separate ways. Jin is a central figure in the story, since he has the ability to travel through time, and he wants to save his friends from suffering or pain.

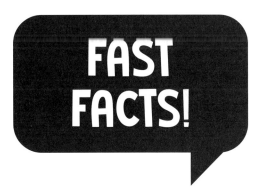

FAST FACTS!

In 2019, it was announced that Big Hit Entertainment would be producing a television series set in the BU.

Since then, there have been a few details about this TV show that were revealed to the public, the most recent of which were released in 2023. For instance, the title of this still-forthcoming TV drama is *Youth*.

To the Future!

After ten years of nonstop singing, dancing, rapping, songwriting, recording, performing, and touring as BTS, the group released the song "Take Two" on June 9, 2023, to commemorate their tenth anniversary.

But this anniversary was bittersweet, because the year before that—in 2022—the Bangtan Boys' forthcoming mandatory military service (and desire to focus on solo projects) forced BTS to temporarily press pause on their careers as an idol group. However, Big Hit Entertainment has said that the group is hoping to start making music again roughly around 2025.

What does the future hold for BTS? It's difficult to know for certain.

But throughout their careers as an idol group, the boys have crafted songs that were increasingly ambitious and increasingly personal. They've taken chances creatively, addressing real-world issues when their contemporaries shied away from doing so. If that's any indication of the path that lies ahead for them, the future of BTS is very bright indeed!

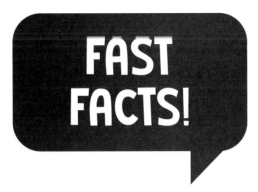

FAST FACTS!

South Korean male citizens are obligated to enlist for eighteen months of military service before they turn thirty years old.

In May 2023, BTS released a new digital single titled "The Planet," which was part of the soundtrack for the animated television series *Bastions*.

Did You Know That . . .

1 In the television drama *Youth*, the members of BTS will not be appearing on camera.

2 In other words, there will be seven actors *playing* the boys of BTS.

3 This makes sense, since technically, the Bangtan Universe narrative is about fictional characters *inspired by* the members of BTS.

4 *Youth* will be about how these seven characters first met.

5 But it's important to note that the storylines and characters depicted in *Youth* are fictional, and don't reflect the actual lives or experiences of the members of BTS.

6 *Bastions* is an environmentally themed series about a group of superheroes.

7 In *Bastions*, the villains try to pollute the Earth.

8 In November 2021, BTS resumed in-person concerts after canceling live performances due to the pandemic in early 2020.

9 During the pandemic, they did hold some online concerts.

10 In October 2022, a few months after announcing that they were taking a break from performing as a group, BTS performed an emotionally charged concert in Busan, South Korea.

Warmth and Comfort

"The moment we meet our ARMYs who know us and love us is like coming home and feeling all its warmth and comfort."

—J-Hope speaking about BTS's loyal fanbase

Who—or what—gives *you* warmth and comfort? It could be your parents, your siblings, your friends, a stuffed animal you keep on your bed, your favorite musical instrument, or a cherished family photograph from long ago. Write about it on the lines below.

_____

_____

_____

_____

_____

_____

_____

_____

_____

_____

_____

_____

_____

_____

_____

_____

_____

_____

_____

_____

Tell Your Story

The Bangtan Universe tells one long, sprawling story spread out over various music videos, a webtoon, a book, a mobile game, and more. The BU involves the story of seven friends, but it also involves time travel. If you were able to tell one long, interconnected story like the BU does, what would your story be about? Who would the characters be? What would they do? Write about your story on the lines below.

_____

_____

_____

_____

_____

_____

_____

_____

_____

_____

_____

_____

_____

_____

_____

_____

_____

ANSWER KEY

Pages 18–19:
1) c, 2) a, 3) d, 4) b, 5) a

Pages 34–35:
1) c, 2) b, 3) a, 4) c, 5) d

Pages 50–51:
1) a, 2) b, 3) c, 4) d, 5) a

Pages 66–67:
1) b, 2) a, 3) d, 4) b, 5) d

ABOUT THE AUTHOR

Arie Kaplan began his career writing about pop music for magazines such as *Teen Beat*, *Tiger Beat*, and *BOP*. And over the years, he has satirized pop music as a writer for *MAD Magazine*. Arie is also the author of the juvenile nonfiction book *American Pop: Hit Makers, Superstars, and Dance Revolutionaries*.

As a nonfiction author, Arie is perhaps most well-known for the acclaimed book *From Krakow to Krypton: Jews and Comic Books*, a 2008 finalist for the National Jewish Book Award. He has also penned numerous books and graphic novels for young readers, including *LEGO Star Wars: The Official Stormtrooper Training Manual*, *The New Kid from Planet Glorf*, *Jurassic Park Little Golden Book*, *Frankie and the Dragon*, and *Swashbuckling Scoundrels: Pirates in Fact and Fiction*. Aside from his work as an author, Arie is a screenwriter for television, video games, and transmedia. Please check out his website: www.ariekaplan.com.